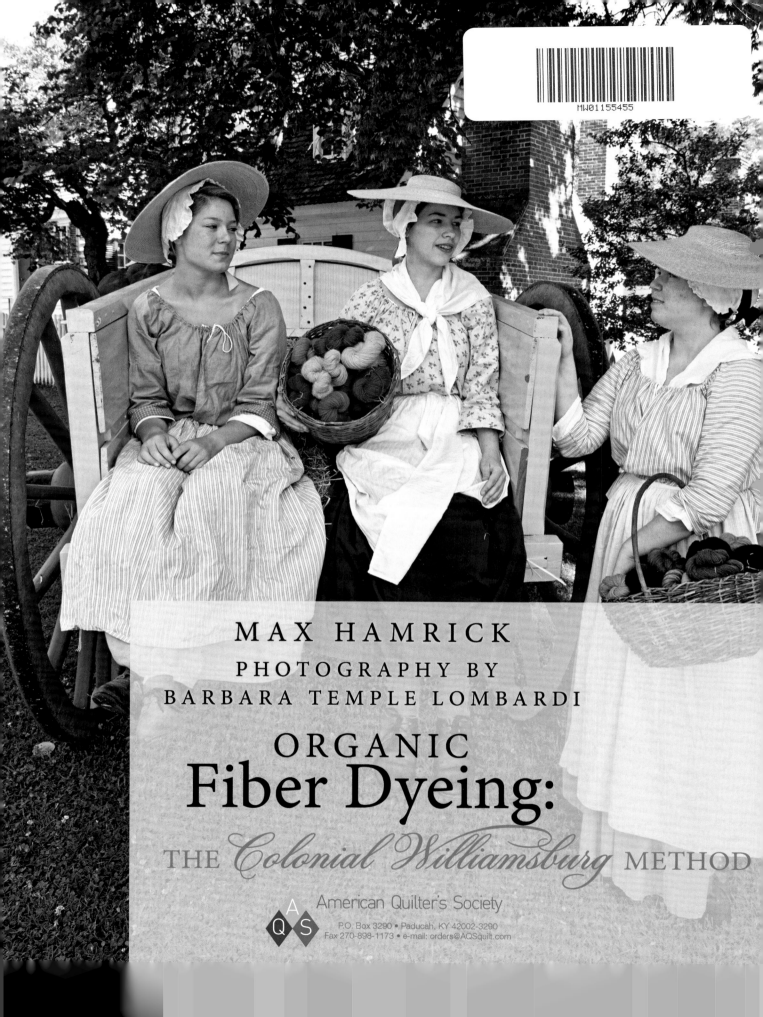

MAX HAMRICK

PHOTOGRAPHY BY
BARBARA TEMPLE LOMBARDI

ORGANIC
Fiber Dyeing:
THE *Colonial Williamsburg* METHOD

American Quilter's Society
P.O. Box 3290 • Paducah, KY 42002-3290
Fax 270-898-1173 • e-mail: orders@AQSquilt.com

Located in Paducah, Kentucky, the American Quilter's Society (AQS) is dedicated to promoting the accomplishments of today's quilters. Through its publications and events, AQS strives to honor today's quiltmakers and their work and to inspire future creativity and innovation in quiltmaking.

EXECUTIVE BOOK EDITOR: ELAINE BRELSFORD
BOOK EDITOR: KATHY DAVIS
COPY EDITOR: CHRYSTAL ABHALTER
GRAPHIC DESIGN: ELAINE WILSON
COVER DESIGN: MICHAEL BUCKINGHAM
PHOTOGRAPHY: BARBARA TEMPLE LOMBARDI, UNLESS OTHERWISE NOTED

Additional copies of this book may be ordered from the American Quilter's Society, PO Box 3290, Paducah, KY 42002-3290, or online at www.AmericanQuilter.com.

Text and Photography © 2013, The Colonial Williamsburg Foundation
Design © 2013, American Quilter's Society

American Quilter's Society
P.O. Box 3290 • Paducah, KY 42002-3290
Fax 270-898-1173 • e-mail: orders@AQSquilt.com

LIBRARY OF CONGRESS CONTROL NUMBER: 2013942832

Acknowledgments

I want to say "Thanks" to a very extraordinary teacher. I met him when I was a junior in high school. He was a new teacher then, maybe six years older than me. He taught business curriculum. He helped me to understand that learning was essential to life and that studying and doing research were essential to learning. He gave of his time and knowledge, far beyond any requirements of his employment. His gentle instruction and kind tutoring left me with a lifelong facility to study and learn. He has remained my friend for nearly half a century.

Thank you, Mr. Richardson.

Contents

OPPOSITE: Photo by Tom Green

Introduction

In 1988, when I started working in the Colonial Williamsburg Foundation's Spinning, Weaving, and Dyeing Shop, part of my job was to put together dye programs. These programs needed to be true to the reality of eighteenth-century English and Virginia textile coloring, as well as safe for humans, animals, and the environment. This created a quandary. In the world of eighteenth-century England, there were few regulations governing dangerous chemicals, and many dye recipes from that time contain substances that are unsafe.

Fortunately, I also found plenty of sources for dyes that are completely suitable for today's dyers. I drew from a range of eighteenth-century sources: dictionaries, encyclopedias, how-to books, newspaper advertisements and articles, as well as notebooks and personal papers of those practicing the dyers' trade. A tremendous amount of information on eighteenth-century fiber coloring has made the trip through time, and this book is not by any means comprehensive or definitive.

I have selected dye recipes that are fairly simple yet true to the reality of eighteenth-century English and Virginia dyeing. I also tried to limit the ingredients in these recipes, while allowing you to create an abundant range of colors and shades.

Besides the recipes themselves, I hope this book will also give you awareness of why dyeing was practiced in eighteenth-century Virginia; of the methods, tools, and utensils employed in doing so; and of dyestuffs used by the Virginians to obtain a wide range of colors and shades.

A tremendous amount of information on eighteenth-century fiber coloring has made the trip through time…

Dyeing in Virginia

*T*oday, every store that sells clothing has racks full of garments in lots of colors and shades. If you don't think you look good in red, buy green or blue; they all cost the same. The question of how it got that color seldom, if ever, crosses a consumer's mind.

Dyeing was not that advanced in seventeenth- and eighteenth-century England, but it was already highly developed. The existence of the trade of dyeing was noted as early as 1188. In 1310–1311, the "Worshipful Company of Dyers" was given the powers of self-regulation. Its first royal charter was issued in 1471.[1]

English history of the seventeenth and eighteenth centuries is rich with laws pertaining to substances that were used to color textiles. Some were very specific; for example, a 1662 act for the importing of madder stated, among other things, the strict penalties of fines and forfeiture should madder be discovered to be diluted with sand.

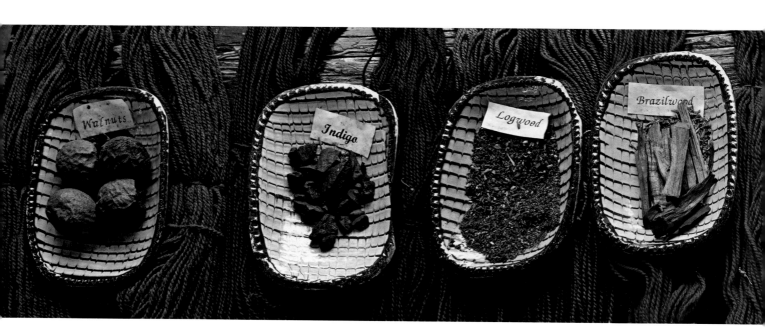

The dyeing process, circa 1762–1772. Illustration by Denis Diderot.

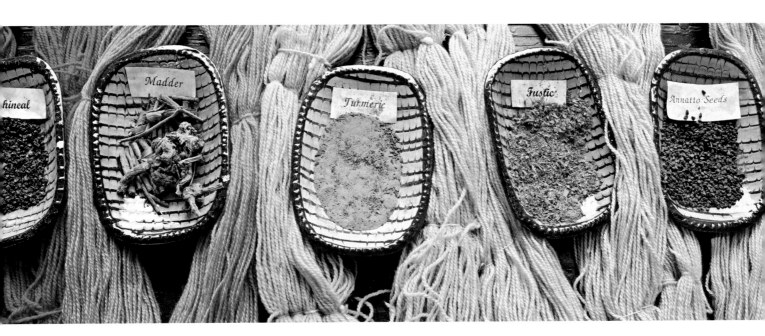

That if any person or persons shall from and after the Foure and twentieth day of June in the yeare of our Lord One thousand six hundred sixty and two import into this Realm of England or any part thereof any Madder whatsoever or expose the same to sale being mixed with sand or other materials over and above two pound weight in every hundred weight of Madder which hundred weight shall containe One hundred and twelve pound that then every person and persons so offending as aforesaid shall forfeit and lose all and every such parcell of Madder so mixed with sand or other materials as afore said the one moyetie (half) of the said forfeiture to be to the use of His Majesty His Heires and Successors and the other moiety (half) to such person or persons as shall discover the same to be recovered by him by Action or Bill of Debt in any of His Majesties Courts of Westminster wherein no Essoign Protection or Wager of Law shall be allowed.[2]

The English colonists at Jamestown were much less sophisticated in their dyeing techniques. Partly this was because England, recognizing the importance of its textile industry, prohibited those with expertise from leaving.

Written records pertaining to local natural dyes that could document the varieties or amounts of each used in seventeenth- and eighteenth-century Virginia have not made their way through time. However, dyes are mentioned as early as 1608, when the Council of Virginia included dyes of sundry sorts and rich value among the colony's staple and certain commodities.[3]

The English had high hopes that imports from their New World colonies might allow them to end their dependence on Spain and Holland for certain dyestuffs. Although dyes never became a significant Virginia export, early colonists did experiment with native flowers, berries, nuts, leaves, stems, bark, and roots. Tobacco simply proved to be too profitable to allow for further experimenting and development of other products, such as dye.

By the mid-eighteenth century, tobacco had brought enough wealth to Virginia that many were no longer content with a simple subsistence. People knew that to do well, you must appear to be doing well. It was imperative to be dressed in the proper clothes.

Textiles were needed for every facet of life. Inventories of Virginia stores reveal that 60 to 80 percent of the items for sale were textiles or textile-related. Of the town's craftsmen and artisans, 36 percent were in businesses involving textiles. This represents the largest occupational grouping in Williamsburg, outnumbering metalworkers (the second largest) by more than two to one. However, most cloth was shipped from England. Even during the American Revolution when Virginians were cut off from almost all English goods, cloth manufacturing in Williamsburg is documented only at the edge of town, not within the city limits.

The average citizen of eighteenth-century Virginia was most likely not familiar with the

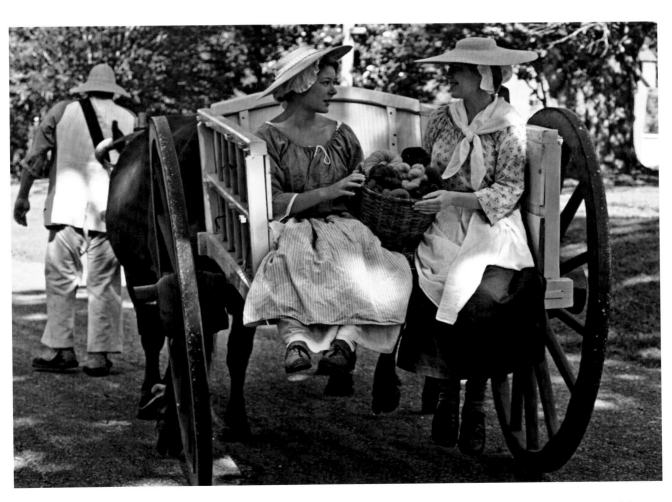

technical processes involved in coloring cloth, but it was common knowledge that some colors cost a good deal more than others. In many cases, the color someone wore was an economic indicator of the household or family he or she represented. Therefore, discoveries and innovations in the science of coloring textiles were news and sometimes made the front page of newspapers throughout the English-speaking world, as did a June 10, 1773, announcement in *The Virginia Gazette* of experiments with the art of dyeing linen scarlet.

> We hear that the art of dying linen yarn scarlet has arrived at a singular degree of perfection if not its new plus ultra, as it rather exceeds than falls short of woolen ditto in point of color and duration by the steady perseverance and judicious experiments of a young man in the dying business in New Castle.

The vast majority of cloth making in Virginia before the American Revolution took place on large plantations.

Slaves had no choice but to wear what they were given. Why then, go to the trouble of coloring anything for them? In many cases, runaways from a particular plantation are described in newspaper ads as being dressed in clothes of the same or similar colors. Perhaps some plantation owners "color coded" clothing in an attempt to easily distinguish which slaves belonged to them.

Most slave owners that were practicing dyeing opted to do the kind of dyeing we associate today with folk art. The dyestuffs used produced earth-tone colors for the most part. Dyes were made from tree barks, nuts, leaves, roots, and galls (abnormal outgrowths of plant tissues). The plantation dyer could get nearly everything he needed in nearby woods, and a few dye plants such as madder were easily grown in a kitchen or herb garden. Common knowledge and common sense aided plantation dyers more than technology and professional training.

On July 8, 1737, a *Virginia Gazette* advertisement documents William Dubberley, hatter, practicing a second trade in dyeing in Williamsburg, saying of Dubberley, *"He also dresses old Hats, very well; and dyes Silks, Wool, and Woollens, at reasonable rates."*

Throughout Virginia, the practice of professional dyeing was rare until the colony began to move toward revolution. Even artisans who could be documented practicing the trade of dyeing usually plied another trade as well. Sometimes artisans plying another trade practiced dyeing, too.[4] Craftsmen involved in dyeing cloth often did clothes washing, cleaning, fulling, finishing, and fancy pressing.[5]

For these artisans, changing the color of a cloth used to construct a lady's gown or a man's three-piece suit was a way to add to their livelihoods. Eighteenth-century dyers used state-of-the-art dyes to produce the bright colors that were the fashion of the era.

Most of the dyes used by Virginia's professional dyers came from England. England bought many of them from Spain which obtained them from her colonies in Central and South America. These dyes were expensive. Many dye substances had more than one use and were readily available in Virginia stores. Store advertisements, probate inventories, journals, and ledgers from eighteenth-century Virginia inform us that cochineal, fustic, indigo, logwood, madder, turmeric, brazilwood, and walnuts were all available in Virginia stores.

As the Revolution approached and Virginians began thinking about independence, they also gradually became more independent in their approach to textiles in general and dyeing in particular. By mid-1766, there was enough displeasure with England to warrant earnest attempts at textile manufacturing in Virginia. In July 1766, Mathew Dick ran an ad for a business whose whole existence depended on textile manufacturing, including dyeing:

"I ACQUAINT the public that I have settled at Mr. Samuel Du Val's in Henrico County, where I purpose to carry on the FULLING business in the best and cheapest manner ever done in this colony, the mill, the dies, & ect. Being now ready, and in the best order; the wool from the neck and shoulders is the best for the finest cloth; all woolen cloth should be wove at least 5 quarters wide. Cloth will be milled, & ect. from four pence to one shilling and six pence per yard. All those who will favor me with their custom, if they will send their cloth to the mill to Rocket's landing or to Westham, it shall be received, and milled, & ect. in the neatest manner, and with the greatest dispatch, and their directions most punctually observed and followed, by the public's most obedient humble servant."

The connections between textile manufacturing and the coming Revolution became clearer in a 1769 ad placed in *The Virginia Gazette* by John Turerville and Francis Lightfoot Lee, a future signer of the Declaration of Independence. In June 1770, Benjamin Brooks, who may have been hired by Turerville and Lee to operate their fulling mill, placed an ad that said:

> This mill was erected principally with a view of encouraging our manufactures at this time, when the use of goods imported from our mother country is utterly destructive of our liberty.

What follows are all the known *Virginia Gazette* advertisements placed by dyers. The advertisements are in chronological order and illustrate the increasing importance of textile coloring in Virginia as independence approached.

Some of these advertisements ran in more than one publisher's *Virginia Gazette*. (There was sometimes more than one newspaper published under that same name.) Some of them ran in the same publisher's *Virginia Gazette* more than one time.

These first two are the only advertisements for a craftsman doing cloth dyeing found in any *Virginia Gazette* from a time before Virginians began thinking about independence. William Dubberley was a hatter practicing a second trade in dyeing.

WILLIAM DUBBERLEY, Hatter,

HAS lately set up the Trade of Hat-making, in Williamsburg; by whom Gentlemen, and others, may be supply'd at very reasonable Rates, with the following Sorts of Hats, viz. Mens Beavers, of any Fashion or Size; Womens Beavers, White, Black, Shagg'd, or otherwise; and Castors of the best and neatest Sort. He also buys Beaver Furr, Raccoon, Fox, Muskrat, and Hare Skins, and will give Encouragement to any Persons that will supply him with such. He also dresses old Hats, very well; and dyes Silks, Wool, and Woollens, at reasonable Rates. Enquire for the said William Dubberley, at Mr. John Mundell's, in Williamsburg.

Source: *Virginia Gazette* (Purdie) July, 8, 1737, page 4

THIS is to give Notice, That William Dubberly, Hatter, continues the Trade of Hat-making, in the City of Williamsburg; by whom, Gentlemen and Others may be furnished with extraordinary good Beaver Hats, fit for any Service; Beaverets and Castors, very good and cheap. Likewise, Womens Hats, white or black, shag'd, or otherwise: He will engage the Dye to hold a reasonable Time, as well as any European Hats whatever. He also dyes any manner of Woollens and Silks, Silk Stockings, & c. free from Rotting, or the least Impairing. He likewise buys Beaver, Raccoon, and Hares Furs, and will give good Encouragement to Those that will supply him with such, provided they are caught in the Winter Quarter. Those Gentlemen that please to make Use of him in any of the above Premises, may depend upon honest and faithful Usage, by their

Humble Servant,
William Dubberly

Source: *Virginia Gazette* (Purdie) September 21, 1739, page 4

By mid-1766, there was enough displeasure with the mother country to warrant earnest attempts at textile manufacturing in Virginia. There was a fulling mill in Augusta County in 1751.[6] Sometime before 1765, John Wily and John Sutton operated a fulling mill in Caroline County that was for sale in March of 1772.[7]

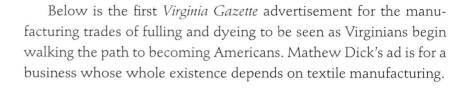

Below is the first *Virginia Gazette* advertisement for the manufacturing trades of fulling and dyeing to be seen as Virginians begin walking the path to becoming Americans. Mathew Dick's ad is for a business whose whole existence depends on textile manufacturing.

I ACQUAINT the public that I have settled at Mr. Samuel Du Val's in Henrico County, where I purpose to carry on the FULLING business in the best and cheapest manner ever done in this colony, the mill, the dies, & ect. Being now ready, and in the best order; the wool from the neck and shoulders is the best for the finest cloth; all woolen cloth should be wove at least 5 quarters wide. Cloth will be milled, & ect. from four pence to one shilling and six pence per yard. All those who will favor me with their custom, if they will send their cloth to the mill to Rocket's landing or to Westham, it shall be received, and milled, & ect. in the neatest manner, and with the greatest dispatch, and their directions most punctually observed and followed, by the public's most obedient humble servant

MATHEW DICK

Sources: *Virginia Gazette* (Purdie & Dixon) July 4, 1766, page 3
Virginia Gazette (Purdie & Dixon) July 11, 1766, page 3
Virginia Gazette (Purdie & Dixon) July 18, 1766, page 4

The first of the following advertisements was published three times in September 1769. Almost nine months later, the second advertisement appeared. The first ads were placed by John Turerville and Francis Lightfoot Lee. The last ad carries the name of Benjamin Brooks. We can speculate that Mr. Brooks had been hired by the aforementioned Mr. Turerville and Mr. Lee to operate this fulling mill.

JUST FINISHED, THE Nomony FULLING-MILL, at the Nomony river, in Westmoreland county; where all the different branches of FULLING, DRESSING, SHEARING, and DYEING, will be executed in the best manner and at the most reasonable rates. As the subscribers have been at a considerable expense in producing the materials complete, and a Fuller perfectly acquainted with the business, it is expected that those who favor the mill with their custom, will, when they send for their cloth, send money to pay for it; the profits of a fulling-mill being by no means sufficient to support the expense of keeping accounts, and collecting small debts. The particular sums may be known from the Fuller, when the cloth is sent to the mill.

JOHN TURERVILLE
FRANCES LIGHTFOOT LEE

Sources: *Virginia Gazette* (Rind) September 7, 1769, page 3

Virginia Gazette (Rind) September 14, 1769, page 3

Virginia Gazette (Purdie & Dixon) September 21, 1769, page 3

WESTMORLAND, May 10, 1770

The Nomony FULLING-MILL under my care, being now completely fitted all those who are pleased to favor her with their custom, may depend upon having their cloth finished with the utmost expedition, and in the neatest manner. Though the prices hitherto charged, were agreeable to the custom of the northern colonies, yet as this mill was erected principally with a view of encouraging our own manufactures at this time, when the use of British is utterly destructive of our liberty, therefore the following low rates will for the future be charged, and it is expected the money will be sent when the cloth is taken away, otherwise the mill will by no means support herself. For fulling, 4d per yard, dyeing all shades drab, 2d, per yard. Other colors 4d, except fine greens and blues, which are more costly; shearing 2d, per yard each time the shears go over the cloth, which must depend upon on the fineness of the cloth, and the use it is intended for.

It is impossible to make good work, unless the cloth has been properly managed before it is sent to the mill. The following directions, if complied with, will enable me to give that satisfaction to my customers, of which I am very desirous.

Separate the fine parts of the fleece (which are the neck, shoulders, back and sides) from the course; spin the warp as hard as possible, but of an even hardness: the filling very loose and even; Never spin course wool into fine thread; the cloth will always be harsh; the least width should be as ell; cloths intended to be dyed, must be kept clear of spots or stains; they will always show.

We dye and dress jeans and fustians to look as well as those from England Wool and cotton dyed in grain of any color. Those who favor us with their work are desired to write fully how they would have it done.

BENJAMIN BROOKS

Sources: *Virginia Gazette* (Rind) June 14, 1770, page 3, column 3
Virginia Gazette (Purdie & Dixon) June 14, 1770, page 3, column 2

JOSEPH NORTHUP, silk dyer, late from Boston acquaints all Ladies and Gentlemen, and the public in general, that he has taken a house near the American coffeehouse, in Churchstreet, Norfolk, where he intends to carry on the said business in all its various branches, silks, scarlet, stockings, ribbands, cloaks, &c of what ever kind, and takes off the spots and makes them look as if they were new. He also dresses and presses the country made cloths and stuffs, and dyes cottons and linens at the most reasonable rates, and with the utmost expedition and care.

JOSEPH NORTHUP

Source: *Virginia Gazette* (Rind) March 13, 1772, page 3, column 1

JOSEPH NORTHUP
SILKDYER and SCOWERER

In CHURCH STREET, Norfolk, BEGS leave to acquaint the public that he has set up the business of colouring and scowering SILKS, CLOTHES, FUSTIANS, VIRGINIA CLOTH, and other stuffs, and has got both hot and cold presses for dressing them equal to any done at home; likewise clear starches white silk, and silk stockings, and takes spots out of all kinds of women's wear, at the most reasonable rates, and with the greatest care and expedition.

Source: *Virginia Gazette* (Rind) October 8, 1772, page 3, column 1

The next three advertisements were placed by Elisha and Robert White. The first ad in September 1775 indicates a location near Newcastle, Virginia. The other two ads, placed in December 1775, and December 1776, respectively seem to be for an establishment in Hanover County, Virginia. In the advertisement of December 1775, the Whites give instructions on how to make cloth of cotton and wool yarns twisted together.

The subscribers having erected a fulling mill and being disappointed in the workmen they expected, take this method of enquiring for such as understand the management of a fulling mill, and dyeing and dressing cloth; also good weavers. Such workmen will meet with good encouragement by applying soon to the subscribers near Newcastle.

ELISHA and ROBERT WHITE

Source: *Virginia Gazette* (Pinkney) September 14, 1775, page 3

Hanover County, December 20, 1775

The subscribers have got their fulling mill at work, where the public shall be faithfully and expeditiously served. As a wish to be of service to our community had some weight with us in setting up our works, we think it our duty to inform our countrymen that we have tried some experiments which we conceive will prove of great service, especially to those who have few sheep, and but little wool. A cotton chain filed in with a thread of cotton and a thread of wool, slack twisted together, thickens very well in the mill, and we believe will weave exceeding well. It will make very good winter ware for servants and children. A cotton chain filled in with wool of two pounds and a half of white to one pound of black, will make very good and hansom mixed cloth; fit for any body. The filling should be even spun, and slack twisted. Such cloth should be thin slayed and 5 quarters wide as it shrinks in width only.

Every one who would wish to make good cloth, and have it look well, must be careful to have their wool well mixed, and spun with as even a twist as may be. The chain should be well twisted, the filling courser, of the finest wool, and slack twist. The wool should be sorted as it comes off the sheep. The Belly and the neck is the finest, the sides next, and the shoulders and the thighs the courser. We are prepared for weaving cloth 5 quarters wide, but are at a loss, at present for weavers. If any such, who understands the woolen business, will apply, they will be met with good encouragement.

We are the public's obedient humble servants
ELISHA and ROBERT WHITE

Source: *Virginia Gazette* (Pinkney) December 20, 1775, page 4, column 2

HANOVER FULLING – MILL

At our woolen manufactory are wanted good WOOLEN WEAVERS, also a Man who understands Dyeing and Shearing, where Gentlemen may be served in the best and most expeditious manner, by their humble Servants

ELISHA & ROBERT WHITE

Source: *Virginia Gazette* (Dixon & Hunter) December 13, 1776, page 3

A COMPLETE FULLING MILL is now finishing on Lansdown mill-dam in Richmond county, where all manner of fulling, shearing, pressing, and dyeing, will be performed, on the most reasonable terms, by

LAWRANCE McKINNY

Sources: *Virginia Gazette* (Purdie) April 12, 1776, page 3
Virginia Gazette (Purdie) April 19, 1776, page 1
Virginia Gazette (Purdie) April 26, 1776, page 4
Virginia Gazette (Dixon & Hunter) April 27, 1776, page 4

THIS is to give notice, that we have rented the FULLING MILL in Chesterfield county, on Swift creek, near Petersburg, formerly kept by Richard Jackson and William Bragg, where we do intend carrying on the FULLING, WEAVING and DYING business; also, any person may have old clothes dyed. All persons that will please to favor us with their custom may depend on having their work done in the best and cheapest manner, for ready money only.

JOHN STORY
SAMUEL DEVENPORT

Source: *Virginia Gazette* (Purdie) October 18, 1776, page 2, column 3

The gentlemen placing the advertisement below seem to be in the business of making machinery for the manufacture of yarn and cloth. The ad would lead the reader to believe that they are willing to travel to the far reaches of the colonies to secure work teaching many of the textile trades. It is noteworthy that they advertise:

We have also for sale SPINNING MACHINES, that will spin a pound in an hour of 8 yard thread, to work with any number of spindles, from 10 to 100, just as people choose to have them.

Source: *Virginia Gazette* (Purdie) January, 17, 1777, page 4, column 2

The spinning jenny, basically a multi-spool spinning wheel, was invented in the northwest of England by James Hargreaves in 1764. History records the first water-powered spinning machinery in the former colonies (by then the United States of America) in Pawtucket, Rhode Island, was circa 1790.

Fredericksburg, January 1, 1777

WHEREAS the mystery of SPINNING and WEAVING is so very little known, and so badly practiced, in this and all other parts of America, we the subscribers, think proper to inform the publick what kind of goods we are capable of manufacturing, viz. Cottons of all sorts, jeans, pillows, thicksets, velvet, velveret, baragon jeans, calicoes, muslins, German, French, and common stripes, Dutch cords, corded dimities, corderoys, royal ribs, denims, satinets, Indian jeans, jennets, drawboys, quiltings, figured work of all sorts, linens of any fineness worked to the greatest perfection, plain and striped checks of all sorts, linen and cotton hollands, lawns and cambricks, gowns of any pattern, silk, cotton, and linen, wove to the greatest perfection, woolen cloth of all sorts, fine and coarse, with many other articles too tedious to mention. We have also for sale SPINNING MACHINES, that will spin a pound in an hour of 8 yard thread, to work with any number of spindles, from 10 to 100, just as people choose to have them. These machines spin wool to the greatest perfection; and we are now erecting one of a new construction, which cannot fail to satisfy every one that is desirous to improve in carrying on their family work. We propose raising a number of subscriptions, that the art may be made more publick, and shall teach both to spin and weave; so that if any gentlemen choose to encourage these branches of business, either in town or country, we are ready and willing at any time, or at any distance, to assist, and condition for any number of years, to teach weaving, spinning, shearing, dressing, dying, and fulling, in the greatest perfection. We have an exceeding good hand along with us that understands dying and fulling perfectly well, and have two spinning machines and three pair of looms, with other things ready for carrying on the business, which we can carry along with us into any part of the country, and so be ready to begin business without loss of time, which will be a double advantage to any master of a factory. We have been in this town near 12 months, and are not engaged to any one, but are at our liberty to be called to any part of America, if any gentleman chooses to encourage us; so that we shall always be ready and willing to do all we can for the good of the country, in carrying on every thing both in spinning and weaving. So if any one is desirous to see our works, they may find us in the factory at Fredericksburg, either by writing or in person.

Giles Higson, John Higson, William Paton, Andrew Robinson, William Harwood, William Wilkie

Source: *Virginia Gazette* (Purdie) January 17, 1777, page 4, column 2

Dyeing in Virginia

In the summer of 1777, Robert Carter of Nomini Hall, who operated the largest and longest lasting of the plantation cloth manufactories in Virginia, contracted with Giles Higson and Company to build and operate a textile manufactory as well as purchase looms and spinning machines for it. We find that Giles Higson, his son John Higson, and William Paton had arrived for work at Carter's Aries location in Westmorland County, Virginia, in August, 1777.[8]

I AM in Want of a Person who understands the DYING and FULLING Branches. Such a One, with a recommendation for his Sobriety and Diligence, will meet with extraordinary Encouragement, and constant Employ, by applying to me in Nansemond.

SAMUEL BRADLEY

Source: *Virginia Gazette* (Dixon & Hunter) October 4, 1776, page 4
Virginia Gazette (Dixon & Hunter) January 31, 1777, page 8

THE Subscriber, having been regularly bred to the printing and dying of Linen and Cotton in Dublin, intends to carry on that Business at the Fulling-Mill in Lunenburg. He prints blue and white Handkerchiefs, Gowns, and Counterpanes, and dyes Cotton and Flax Thread, and Fustian of a Mazarine Blue. And as soon as he can procure a good Assortment of Die-Stuffs, he intends to stamp Colours, Cotton, Linen, or Silk Handkerchiefs, of any Colours that may be required. Those who choose to favour him with their Custom may depend upon the Work being done in the best Manner, and upon the most reasonable Terms.

ANDREW DUN

Source: *Virginia Gazette* (Dixon) October 31, 1777, page 2, column 2

Dyeing Tools

A dyeing operation requires large quantities of water; a dyer needs good access to clean water. A dye house or any textile fulling or finishing business would also have great need of the products of a cooper, such as buckets, washtubs, and barrels, etc. A dyer also needs a source of heat. In eighteenth-century Virginia that meant wood to burn. Some of a dyer's most important tools were the pots and kettles. A copper pot generally brightened the luster and color a bit. An iron pot generally saddened it. Depending on what kind and how much fiber was to be dyed, the size of the vessels could range from very small to very large and anywhere in between. A scale was needed to weigh the dyestuffs and additives.

In 1808, during the bankruptcy of a large dye house in Blackley, England[9], the following dyeing utensils were listed for sale:

Twelve lead vats, a valuable assortment of various sized copper pans, a horse wheel and gearing, six large drying stoves, a chopping machine for madder roots, a madder mill, a large number of chemical and dyeing tubs, a quantity of lead pipes and crocks, sundry wringing posts, and drying racks. On June 7 of the same year, many of these items were listed again, indicating that they did not sell the first time. There were a few additional items that would have been of interest to dyers: iron vats, lead and wood cisterns, yarn poles, sundry drains, sieves, scoops, and buckets.[10]

Dyeing Tools

For the recipes in this book, I recommend the following:

- ✠ a metal ceramic-lined pot that will hold 3 to 5 gallons of liquid
- ✠ a hot plate or gas burner that will boil 3 to 5 gallons of water
- ✠ a kitchen scale
- ✠ two or three plastic buckets for soaking yarn or fiber
- ✠ a stirring stick
- ✠ a drying rack or a place to dry what you dye
- ✠ the textiles to be dyed
- ✠ the dye itself
- ✠ the additives necessary for that dye

Rubber gloves are always a good idea, as is an apron to keep the dye off your clothes. Feel free to experiment with different kinds of cooking vessels (iron, copper, aluminum, or steel). If you are going to go historic and cook outside over an open fire, I recommend a copper kettle over a wood fire for everything except the indigo. An iron kettle will work best with the indigo. Copper will work with indigo, but it will not yield quite as dark a blue as iron. Remember to adjust the recipe for the amount of liquid you will be using and the amount of textile you will be dyeing.

Mordants & Other Dye Additives

Mordant is a derivative of the Latin word *mordere* which means to bite. Mordants are usually mineral salts placed on textile fibers to help dyes hold on. The earliest the *Oxford English Dictionary* places the word *mordant* in a context pertaining to textile dyeing is 1791.

Some eighteenth-century dyes will impart good color to textile fibers without using a mordant (walnuts husks and indigo are two examples), but the majority of dyes discussed in this book require a mordant. Eighteenth-century English and Virginia dyers used a good number of things to fix and enhance colors. In particular, the metal of the pot used—copper, aluminum, or iron—will influence the luster on the textile being dyed.

Alum (specifically potassium alum or hydrated potassium aluminum sulfate) is the mordant used in most of the recipes in this book. It is less toxic than most eighteenth-century mordants. However, it is a chemical that should be kept sealed and in a place safe from pets and children.

All eighteenth-century mordants are toxic to one degree or another. Some are downright unsafe. Make it your business to know what the substance is and how it will affect people, children, animals, and the environment before you open the container. Carefully read the label on any substances that you choose to use in your textile dyeing.

Listed below are some eighteenth-century mordants/fixatives and dye additives:

✢ **Alum** (potash alum, aluminum potassium sulfate): The standard mordant on wool and silk. Alum is not entirely non-toxic; however, it is relatively safe to use.

✢ **Blue Vitriol** (copper sulfate): Poisonous and very toxic; a strong irritant; a mordant used to bring out the greens in dyes. It is also useful in darkening the color a dye will achieve on a textile.

✢ **Chrome** (potassium dichromate): Chrome brightens dye colors and is most often used when dyeing wool. Chrome is one of the most dangerous chemicals used in eighteenth-century dyeing. It should never be inhaled. Gloves need to be worn while working with it. Leftover liquids should be treated as hazardous waste. This is extremely toxic. We recommend you not use it.

✢ **Copperas** (ferrous sulfate): Used in wool dyeing to sadden color and luster. It was also used to make inks. Also known as green vitriol.

✢ **Cream of Tartar** (potassium hydrogen tartrate): Most often used in conjunction with alum and tin mordants on wool and silk.

✢ **Galls:** Outgrowths produced on oak trees, caused by the action of insects mostly of the genus *Cynips*. Oak galls were a good source of tannin for eighteenth-century dyers.

✢ **Glauber's Salt** (sodium sulfate decahydrate): Johann Glauber was the first to artificially produce the salt in or about 1656. Glauber's salt was used by eighteenth-century dyers to help the textile dye evenly and more uniformly.

✢ **Sig or Sigg** (stale human urine): This source of ammonia was used for many things by dyers. It was the catalyst for indigo vats.

✢ **Soda Ash or Washing Soda** (sodium carbonate): This substance is dissolved in water to create an alkaline solution for dyeing blue with indigo.

✢ **Tannin** (acidum tannicum): The most common mordant for cellulose fibers such as cotton and linen. Tannic acid is a specific commercial form of tannin.

✢ **Thiourea dioxide**: A modern reducing agent that is used as a catalyst for indigo dyeing. A substitute for sig.

✢ **Tin** (stannous chloride; salt of tin): Tin will brighten colors of red, orange, and yellow on wool and silk. More than just a little bit of it makes wool and silk brittle. At the end of a dyeing, a pinch of tin added to a dye bath mordanted with alum will brighten wool yarns or cloth. Tin was seldom, if ever, used on cellulose fibers in eighteenth-century dyeing. Like all mordants, it is somewhat toxic.

Dyes & Recipes

Each of the following dyes is presented with

✛ a brief description,

✛ a brief history of its use as a dye, and

✛ a *Virginia Gazette* advertisement that places the particular dye for sale in Virginia.

A few words about safety, which are good in any century:

✛ Many dyes and additives are hazardous to people, animals, and the environment. Know what you are working with and how it may affect you and your surroundings.

✛ Never leave a dye kettle unattended.

✛ Dispose of the by-products and what is left over properly.

For all recipes, it is important to note: The color of wet yarn always appears darker than when it is dry. Once the desired color has been obtained, the yarn should be washed to remove any excess dye. To stay true to the history of the recipe, use mild eighteenth-century soap such as Castile. For convenience in today's world, baby shampoo or Orvus® paste will work well. Rinse the yarn in clean water until the rinse water is clear. Remember that even in washing, rapid changes in temperature will cause your wool yarn to shrink.

Have fun, don't pollute, and if you wish to get anywhere near similar results another time, record what you do step by step.

Annatto: Plate 1456: Bixa Orellana or Anotta from *Botanical Magazine* by William Curtis. London: Printed by Stephen Couchman. 1787.

Annatto
(Bixa orellana)

The botanical name for annatto is *Bixa orellana,* named for the Spanish conquistador Francisco de Orellana who completed the first known navigation of the length of the Amazon River (and died on the river in 1546). The plant travels throughout the world under many names: achiote, annetto annotto, aploppas, aranotto, bija, bixin, lipstick plant, orlean, shambu, roucou, urucú, just to mention a few. The ancient Aztecs called it *achiotl*. The plants have been cultivated throughout Central and South America and the Caribbean Islands since ancient times. This makes it impossible to know its original habitat but Brazil is thought to be likely. Today the plant is cultivated in tropical and subtropical regions throughout the world.

Bixa orellana is an evergreen and is considered either a shrub or a small tree. The trunk can grow up to 10 centimeters in diameter and to a height of 2 to 8 meters. Its green leaves are shiny with reddish veins, a round heart-shaped base, and a pointed tip. The bark is light to dark brown, mostly smooth but often with cracks. The inner bark, which can be seen through those cracks, is pink in color. The sap it produces is orange. Twigs are usually green and have scales ranging from rust red to brown. The plant produces pink flowers and bright red spiny fruit. The inedible fruit is harvested for the red seeds which reside within. These seeds are the source of the textile dye, as well as food coloring.

Throughout its known history, it has had many uses. In the modern world it is one of the most used natural coloring agents for food, producing yellow to red colors. During the eighteenth century, it was used to dye cloth and color food, and native peoples of Central and South America painted their skin with it. Its wood was rubbed together to start fires. The pulp surrounding the seeds was used to treat burns, bleeding, dysentery, gonorrhea, constipation, and fever. All of the ancient Maya scriptures were written using annatto juice as ink. Ancient Maya and Aztec civilizations viewed it as a surrogate for blood and it was considered sacred.

It is mentioned as a textile dye in *The Dyer's Assistant in the Art of Dying Wool and Woolen Goods* by James Haigh, printed by J. Bowling, and sold by Mess Rivington and Son, London.

Two *Virginia Gazette* citations show that annatto was known and used as a textile dye in Virginia during Williamsburg's tenure as capital. In the November 25, 1737 edition, an article mentions achiote in the cargo of the Flora and the Assogues, ships that had arrived near Cadiz in August. In the September 15, 1775 edition, an ad refers to the seeds and roots of the aranatto, which dyes yellow and pompadour colours. The *Oxford English Dictionary* states that the word *pompadour* was first used to indicate a shade of pink in 1762, and that it was from time to time used to specify or express various shades and colors ranging from silvery pink to a deep purplish-brick. Throughout more than two centuries, pompadour's use as a color description has come and gone and come and gone, again and again, for no apparent reason and with no apparent regularity.

Dyeing Buttery Yellow with Annatto

INGREDIENTS

- 1 pound of annatto seeds
- 4 ounces of potassium aluminum sulfate (alum)
- 4 ounces of Glauber's salt
- 1 ounce of cream of tartar
- 15 to 30 gallons of water
- Up to 5 pounds of wool yarn

YARN PREPARATION

Soak the yarn to be dyed in clean water for at least 72 hours. This will thoroughly wet all of the molecules of the yarn and make it receptive to dyeing. Add the alum to 3 to 4 gallons of water at room temperature and mix well. Place the yarn in this mixture and slowly bring it to a very gentle boil for 1 hour. The yarn should stay in this mordant (alum) bath until it is ready to be placed into the dye bath.

MAKING A STRONG DYE BATH

Grind or crush the annatto seeds to a fine powder. Place the ground seeds in 3 to 4 gallons of clean water and mix well for about 1 minute. Allow this mixture to soak for at least 24 hours; then mix vigorously for about 1 minute. Bring the mixture to a gentle boil for at least 1 hour (longer, up to 4 hours, will not hurt and will make a stronger dye). This liquid must be strained to remove the bits and pieces of seed. Line a strainer or a colander with several layers of cheesecloth and pour the liquid through this sieve. The seed particles that are strained out can be tied up in the cheesecloth, made into a "tea bag," and used to strengthen the dye bath later, if needed. To this strained mixture, add 1 ounce of cream of tartar and 4 ounces of Glauber's salt. Mix well for about 1 minute. Bring this mixture back to a gentle boil for about 70 minutes. The liquid is now the dye bath and is ready to receive the yarn. Let it cool before dyeing.

MAKING A WEAKER BUT QUICKER DYE BATH

Grind or crush the annatto seeds to a fine powder. Place the annatto powder in several layers of cheesecloth so that the bits and pieces cannot sift through. Place this tea bag in 3 to 4 gallons of clean water and let soak for at least 24 hours. Boil the solution for at least 1 hour (more if you have time), then remove the tea bag. Save this annatto tea bag; it can be used to make another dye pot that is a little weaker than the first. Add 1 ounce of cream of tartar and 4 ounces of Glauber's salt. Mix well for about 1 minute. Bring back to a boil. The liquid is now the dye bath and ready to be used. It may be necessary to allow this to cool before dyeing.

DYEING

It is important not to temperature-shock the yarn. The temperatures of the alum bath and the dye bath should be about the same when transferring the yarn. Rapid changes in temperature will cause the wool yarn to shrink and felt. When ready to begin dyeing, place the yarn directly from the alum bath into the dye bath and slowly bring it to a gentle boil. Cook the yarn until the desired color is achieved.

Brazilwood
(Caesalpinia echinata)

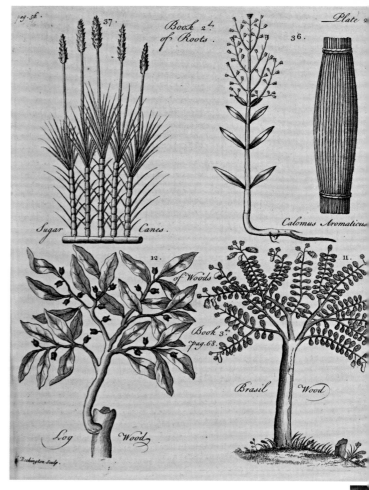

When first introduced to England, brazilwood was the name of the brownish-red wood of the East Indian tree known as sappan *(Cæsalpinia sappan)*, used by textile dyers to obtain a red color. After the discovery of the New World, the name was extended and gradually shifted entirely to the similar wood of a South American species *(Caesalpinia echinata)*. Around 1500 AD, the Portuguese came upon and laid claim to the Atlantic coast of South America between the equator and the Tropic of Capricorn. At first they named this land Terra de Brasil and later Brazil because of the brazilwood trees they found growing there in profusion.

Brazilwood: *A Complete History of Drugs* by Pierre Pomet. London: Printed for J. and J. Bonwicke, S. Birt W. Parker, C. Hitch, and E. Wicksteed. 1747.

Brazilwood yields a red dye on most textiles. The wood is used for making violin bows and high-quality red inks. Its bright red wood is easily turned, can be polished to a bright shine, and was in high demand by cabinetmakers. Its many uses caused it to be logged to near-extinction in the late nineteenth and early twentieth centuries. Today, international trade in the raw wood is regulated. The *Oxford English Dictionary* cites brazilwood's use as a textile dye as early as 1386.

An advertisement in Rind's *Virginia Gazette* of December 4, 1766, states that *The Schooner Polly carrying 13 tons of Brazil-Wood entered in the upper district of the James River on November 25.*

Dyeing Red with Brazilwood

A note about brazilwood as a textile dye: all of the cloth and yarn dyed with brazilwood at Colonial Williamsburg's Weaving, Spinning and Dyeing Shop during the past 22 years began to fade after a few months. Within a few more months, this fading rendered the textile unusable or in need of re-dyeing. We have found this dye to be fugitive in sunlight, water, and the atmosphere. This seemed to be a problem for eighteenth-century dyers, as well. Nonetheless, we are including brazilwood in this study because it is mentioned often in eighteenth-century publications and writings by eighteenth-century dyers.

INGREDIENTS

- ✠ 1 pound of brazilwood chips
- ✠ 6 ounces of potassium aluminum sulfate (alum)
- ✠ 1 ounce of cream of tartar
- ✠ 4 ounces of Glauber's salt
- ✠ 6 to 8 gallons of water
- ✠ Up to 5 pounds of wool yarn

YARN PREPARATION

Soak the yarn to be dyed in clean water for at least 72 hours. This will thoroughly wet all of the molecules of the yarn and make it receptive to dyeing. Add the alum to 3 to 4 gallons of water at room temperature and mix about 30 seconds. Place the yarn in this mixture and slowly bring it to a very gentle boil for 1 hour. The yarn should stay in the mordant (alum) bath until it is ready to be placed into the dye bath. Remember that rapid change in temperature will cause wool yarn to shrink.

MAKING A STRONG DYE BATH

Place the brazilwood in 3 to 4 gallons of clean water and mix well. Allow this mixture to soak for at least 48 hours. Bring the mixture to a boil and let it boil gently for at least 2 hours (a few minutes more will not hurt). This liquid must be strained to remove the brazilwood chips. Line a strainer or colander with several layers of cheesecloth and pour the liquid through this sieve. The brazilwood chips that are strained out can be tied up in the cheesecloth, made into a "tea bag," and used to add strength to the dye bath later, if needed. To the strained dye, add 1 ounce of cream of tartar and 5 ounces of Glauber's salt and mix well for about 1 minute. Bring this mixture back to a gentle boil for about 45 minutes. The liquid is now the dye bath and ready to receive the yarn. It may be necessary to allow this to cool before dyeing.

MAKING A WEAKER DYE BATH

Place the pound of brazilwood chips in several layers of cheesecloth so that the bits and pieces cannot sift through. Place the tea bag in 3 to 4 gallons of clean water. This should soak for at least 24 hours. Next, boil the chips for at least 1 hour; then remove them. Save them as they can be used to make another dye pot that is a little weaker than the first. Add 1 ounce of cream of tartar and 4 ounces of Glauber's salt and mix well for about 1 minute. Bring back to a boil. The liquid is now the dye bath and ready to receive the yarn.

DYEING

It is important not to temperature-shock the yarn. The temperatures of the alum bath and the dye bath should be about the same when transferring the yarn. Rapid changes in temperature will cause the wool yarn to shrink and felt. When ready to do the dyeing, place the yarn directly from the alum bath into the dye bath and slowly bring it to a gentle boil. Cook the yarn until the desired color is achieved.

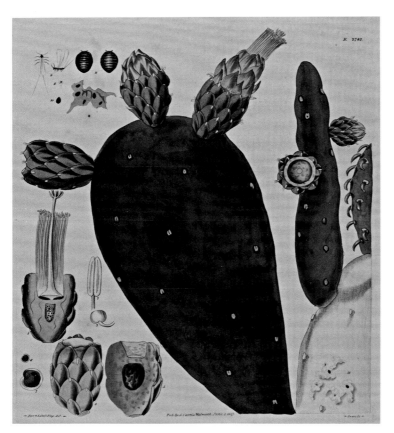

Cochineal: Plate 2742: Cochineal with Cactus from *Botanical Magazine* by William Curtis. London: Printed by Edward Couchman. 1827.

Cochineal
(*Dachtylopious coccus*)

Cochineal, perhaps the most expensive dye used in eighteenth-century Virginia, is made of dried, crushed, and ground insect carcasses. These insects thrive on the cactus *Opuntia cochenillifera*. The female insects, heavily laden with eggs, yield the best dye and are easily harvested from the cactus because they are unable to fly. One pound of cochineal powder for dyeing requires the gathering, drying, crushing, and grinding of 60,000 to 70,000 insects.

The Spanish discovered the natives using cochineal to color cloth when they began to invade and explore Mexico in the sixteenth century. The Spanish found it to be an excellent textile dye and began to market it throughout the known world.[11] Once cochineal's use as a coloring agent was known in Europe, it quickly overtook kermes as the most important red dye.

The English and their colonists found many uses for the powdered insects. Cochineal was used to color leather, food, medicines, paint, and ladies' cheeks and lips. Cochineal yields shades of red ranging from mild pinks to the most vivid of scarlets. The color obtained depends on

the mordant used, the fiber dyed, and the length of time the textile is cooked in the dye.

Asa Ellis gives a detailed description of how cochineal is prepared and used as a textile dye in *A Country Dyer's Assistant*, printed by E. Merriam and Co., Brookfield, Massachusetts, 1798.

Cochineal is one of 72 products advertised by William Pasteur of Williamsburg, Virginia, in Rind's *Virginia Gazette* of September 21, 1769.

APPENDIX.

No. I.

TOTALS

Of an Account of all Rice, Indigo, Cochineal, Tobacco, Sugar, Melaſſes and Rum imported into that Part of Great-Britain called England, for ten Years, ending at Chriſtmas laſt; viz. from Chriſtmas 1772 to Chriſtmas 1782, diſtinguiſhing each Year, the ſeveral Quantities and Species.

RICE Imported into England.

Years	Cwt.	qrs.	lb.
1773	457122	1	23
1774	425359	3	20
1775	577149	0	22
1776	6436	0	27
1777	13016	1	20
1778	11431	0	3
1779	65	0	14
1780	822	3	14
1781	40146	2	12
1782	2716	2	2

COCHINEAL Imported into England.

Years	Pounds Wt.
1773	169245
1774	238415
1775	198053
1776	211147
1777	194159
1778	130255
1779	100891
1780	99057
1781	124566
1782	104216

INDIGO Imported into England.

Years	Pounds Wt.
1773	1518552
1774	1917055
1775	2454811
1776	785671
1777	818458
1778	756798
1779	733730
1780	511549
1781	1032610
1782	569443

TOBACCO Imported into England.

Pounds Wt.

1773.
	Pounds Wt.
Not Prize	55928957
Prize	0 0
Total	55928957

1774.
	Pounds Wt.
Not Prize	56048393
Prize	0 0
Total	56048393

1775.

b

Dyeing Red, Pink and Scarlet with Cochineal

INGREDIENTS

- ✛ 8 ounces of cochineal
- ✛ 4 ounces of potassium aluminum sulfate (alum)
- ✛ 4 ounces of Glauber's salt
- ✛ 1 ounce of cream of tartar
- ✛ 6 to 8 gallons of water
- ✛ Up to 5 pounds of wool yarn

YARN PREPARATION

Soak the yarn to be dyed in clean water for at least 72 hours. This will thoroughly wet all of the molecules of the yarn and make it receptive to dyeing. Add the alum to 3 to 4 gallons of water at room temperature and mix well. Place the yarn in the mixture and slowly bring it to a very gentle boil for 1 hour. The yarn should stay in this mordant (alum) bath until it is ready to be placed into the dye bath.

MAKING A STRONG DYE BATH

Grind or crush the cochineal to a fine powder. Place the ground cochineal in 3 to 4 gallons of clean water and mix well for about a minute. Allow this mixture to soak for at least 24 hours and then mix vigorously for one minute. Bring the mixture to a gentle boil for at least 1 hour (a few minutes more will not hurt). The liquid must be strained to remove the undissolved cochineal powder. Line a strainer or colander with several layers of cheesecloth and pour the liquid through this sieve. The cochineal that is strained out can be tied up in cheesecloth, made into a "tea bag," and used to strengthen the dye bath later, if needed. To this strained mixture, add 1 ounce of cream of tartar and 4 ounces of Glauber's salt. Mix well for about a minute. Bring the mixture back to a gentle boil for about 70 minutes. The liquid is now the dye bath and ready to receive the yarn. It may be necessary to allow this to cool before dyeing.

MAKING A WEAKER DYE BATH

Grind or crush the cochineal to a fine powder. Place the cochineal powder in several layers of cheesecloth so that the bits and pieces cannot sift through. Place this "tea bag" in 3 to 4 gallons of clean water and soak for at least 24 hours. Next, boil the mixture for at least one hour, then remove the tea bag. Save the cochineal tea bag. It can be used to make another dye pot that is a little weaker than the first. Add 1 ounce of cream of tartar and 4 ounces of Glauber's salt. Mix well for about a minute. Bring it back to a boil. The liquid is now the dye bath and ready to be used. It may be necessary to allow this to cool before dyeing.

DYEING

It is important not to temperature-shock the yarn. The temperatures of the alum bath and the dye bath should be about the same when transferring the yarn. Rapid changes in temperature will cause the wool yarn to shrink and felt. When ready to do the dyeing, place the yarn directly from the alum bath into the dye bath and slowly bring it to a gentle boil. Cook the yarn until the desired color is achieved.

Fustic

Fustic: Plate 29. Opp. Pg. 73: Fustick Wood from *A Complete History of Drugs* by Pierre Pomet. London: Printed for J. and J. Bonwicke, S. Birt W. Parker, C. Hitch, and E. Wicksteed. 1747.

Old Fustic *(Chlorophora tinctoria or Maclura tinctoria)* is a yellow dye derived from the heartwood of dyer's mulberry, a large, tropical American tree. *The Oxford English Dictionary* references old fustic as a dye in 1630.

Young Fustic *(Zante fustic or Venetian sumac)* is derived from the wood of the smoke tree *(Cotinus coggygria or Rhus cotinus)*, a southern European and Asian shrub of the cashew family. Young fustic has been used as a dyestuff since antiquity.

Two newspaper advertisements make it clear that fustic was available to eighteenth-century Virginians in both large and small quantities. In the June 10, 1773, Purdie & Dixon *Virginia Gazette*, Mr. John Thomson of Petersburg, Virginia, advertised that he had fustic and several other dyes for sale.

The following notice appeared in Purdie & Dixon's *Virginia Gazette* on January 10, 1777:

Williamsburg, January 7, 1777

By virtue of a decree of the Hon Court of Admiralty of this state, will be sold for ready money, at public venue, in the town of York, twelve miles below the city of Williamsburg, on Monday the 20th instant, the ship Jane, about 120 tuns burthen, with her rigging and tackle, apparel, and furniture; also her cargo, consisting of 79 hogsheads and tierces of BROWN SUGAR, 21 puncheons and 3 barrels of rum, one pipe, 8 hogsheads and 12 quarter casks of very fine Madeira WINE, 13 bales of COTTON, and 80 tuns of FUSTIC, a wood very useful in dyeing. The cargo was shipped at Tortola, and brought here by Capt. Thomas Lilly of the armed brig Liberty. An inventory of rigging, ect. belonging to the ship may be seen by applying to Capt. Lilly, or to the subscriber in this city.

BEN: POWELL; Marshall

Dyeing Yellow with Fustic

Old fustic is the dye of choice, but all eighteenth-century yellow textile dyes are severely fugitive in sunlight. Yarn and cloth dyed with fustic will both sunburn (get darker) and fade unevenly when exposed to sunlight for just a few minutes. Don't dry yellows in sunlight.

INGREDIENTS

- ✛ 10 ounces of fustic chips or sawdust
- ✛ 4 ounces of potassium aluminum sulfate (alum)
- ✛ 1 ounce of cream of tartar
- ✛ 4 ounces of Glauber's salt
- ✛ 6 to 8 gallons of water
- ✛ Up to 5 pounds of wool yarn

YARN PREPARATION

Soak the yarn to be dyed in clean water for at least 72 hours. This will thoroughly wet all of the molecules of the yarn and make it receptive to dyeing. Add the alum to 3 to 4 gallons of water at room temperature and mix well. Place the yarn in this mixture and slowly bring this to a very gentle boil for 1 hour. The yarn should stay in this mordant (alum) bath until it is placed into the dye bath.

MAKING A STRONG DYE BATH

Place the fustic chips or sawdust in 3 to 4 gallons of clean water and mix well for about a minute. Allow the mixture to soak for at least 24 hours, and then mix vigorously for about 1 minute. Bring the mixture to a gentle boil for at least 3 hours (more boiling will not hurt). The liquid must be strained to remove the fustic chips or sawdust. Strain the liquid by pouring it through several layers of cheesecloth. The fustic chips that are strained out can be tied up in the cheesecloth to make a "tea bag" and used to strengthen the dye bath later, if needed. To this strained mixture, add 1 ounce of cream of tartar and 4 ounces of Glauber's salt. Mix well for about 1 minute. Gently boil the solution for about 45 minutes. The liquid is now the dye bath and ready to receive the yarn. It may be necessary to allow this to cool before dyeing.

MAKING A QUICKER, WEAKER DYE BATH

Place the fustic chips or sawdust in several layers of cheesecloth so that the bits and pieces cannot sift through. Place the tea bag in 3 to 4 gallons of clean water. This needs to soak for at least 24 hours. Next, boil the mixture for at least 2 hours; then remove the tea bag which may be used later to strengthen the color of the dye bath, if needed. Add 1 ounce of cream of tartar and 4 ounces of Glauber's salt. Mix well for about 1 minute. Bring the solution back to a boil. The liquid is now the dye bath and ready to be used. Save the fustic tea bag; it can be used to make another dye pot that is a little weaker than the first.

DYEING

It is important not to temperature-shock the yarn. The temperatures of the alum bath and the dye bath should be about the same when transferring the yarn. Rapid changes in temperature will cause the wool yarn to shrink and felt. When ready to do the dyeing, place the yarn directly from the alum bath into the dye bath and slowly bring it to a gentle boil. Cook the yarn until the desired color is achieved.

Turmeric
(*Curcuma longa*)

Tuneric: Plate 1546: Curcuma Zedoaria or Aromatic Turmeric from *Botanical Magazine* by WIlliam Curtis. London: Printed by Stephen Couchman. 1787.

Turmeric is native to the tropics of South Asia. It needs temperatures between about 68°F and about 90°F and a good bit of rainfall to grow well. The turmeric plant generates yellow flowers and an underground stem that produces horizontal roots. These roots, called *rhizomes,* need to be boiled for at least 3 hours, then thoroughly dried and ground into a powder. This powder is used in the preparation of many Indian, Persian, Thai, and Malay foods. Turmeric also has cosmetic and medical uses. *The Oxford English Dictionary* cites turmeric's use as a textile dye in 1621. Turmeric yields shades of yellow on fibers.

Turmeric is one of the few bright dyes used by the English in the eighteenth century that was not a product of the lands within the realm of Spain's empire. As with other eighteenth-century yellow textile dyes, fiber or yarn colored with turmeric is severely fugitive. With just a few minutes of exposure to sunlight, the textile will both sunburn (get darker) and fade unevenly. Most bright yellow garments were, therefore, relegated to nighttime wear. Bright, shiny silks and cottons reflected light and were popular as formal wear in rooms that were lit by candlelight.

An advertisement appearing in a supplement to the Rind *Virginia Gazette* on June 17, 1773, lists turmeric among the many articles available from Mr. John Powell in Richmond.

Dyeing Yellow with Turmeric

INGREDIENTS

- ✛ 10 ounces of turmeric
- ✛ 4 ounces of potassium aluminum sulfate (alum)
- ✛ 1 ounce of cream of tartar
- ✛ 5 ounces of Glauber's salt
- ✛ 6 to 8 gallons of water
- ✛ Up to 5 pounds of wool yarn

YARN PREPARATION

Soak the yarn to be dyed in clean water for at least 72 hours. This will thoroughly wet all of the molecules of the yarn and make it receptive to dyeing. Add the alum and cream of tartar to 3 to 4 gallons of room-temperature water. Place the yarn in this mixture. Bring it to a very gentle boil for 1 hour. The yarn should stay in the mordant (alum) bath until it is ready to be placed into the dye bath.

MAKING A STRONG DYE BATH

Place the turmeric in 3 to 4 gallons of clean water and mix well for about 1 minute. Allow the mixture to soak for at least 24 hours; then mix vigorously for about 1 minute. Bring the mixture to a gentle boil for at least 1 hour; a few minutes more will not hurt. Strain the liquid by pouring it through several layers of cheesecloth. The turmeric that is strained out can be tied up in the cheesecloth to make a "tea bag" and used to strengthen the dye bath later, if needed. To the mixture, add 1 ounce of cream of tartar and 5 ounces of Glauber's salt. Mix well. Bring the mixture back to a boil and boil gently for about 1 hour. The liquid is now the dye bath and ready to receive the yarn. It may be necessary to allow this to cool before dyeing.

MAKING A WEAKER DYE BATH

Place the turmeric in several layers of cheesecloth so that the bits and pieces cannot sift through. Place the turmeric tea bag in 3 to 4 gallons of clean water. This needs to soak for at least 24 hours. Boil the mixture for at least 1 hour. Remove the tea bag and save it to be used to make another dye pot that is a little weaker than the first. Add 1 ounce of cream of tartar and 5 ounces of Glauber's salt. Mix well for about 1 minute. Bring this solution back to a boil. The liquid is now the dye bath and ready to be used. It may be necessary to allow this to cool before dyeing.

DYEING

The temperatures of the alum bath and the dye bath should be about the same when transferring the yarn. Rapid changes in temperature will cause the wool yarn to shrink and felt. When you are ready to do the dyeing, place the yarn directly from the alum bath into the dye bath and slowly bring it to a gentle boil. Cook the yarn until the desired color is achieved.

Remember that all eighteenth-century yellow textile dyes are severely fugitive in sunlight. Fibers dyed with turmeric, as with all eighteenth-century yellow dyes, will both sunburn (get darker) and fade unevenly when exposed to sunlight for just a few minutes. Do not dry your beautiful new yellow yarn in the sun.

Indigo

Indigo: Vol I; Amorpha; Plate XXVII;
*Figures of the most beautiful...Plants...
Three Hundred Copper Plates*; by
Philip Miller; London.

*I*ndigo was introduced to European dyers in the sixteenth century where it quickly became the chief blue dye for fabrics made of wool. However, indigo's use as a dye in the area now known as India dates to a time before most things were recorded in writing. We know this from cloth samples that have survived, as well as drawings on Egyptian, Chinese, and Mayan tombs.

The dye was obtained primarily from the plants of the *indigofera* family. The coloring agent is obtained from the plant's leaves by a process of fermentation. The dye was easily transported in small charcoal-like briquettes of mud removed from the bottom of the working vats after evaporation and drying. These mud briquettes are referred to as "junks."

The origins of indigo are not known. The plants thrived in Central and South America within the realm of Spain's conquest. These areas were the leading producers of indigo during the time leading up to the American Revolution. Indigo was, however, a major cash crop in the colony of South Carolina during the eighteenth century. Indigo growth was a huge and successful industry until it was synthesized late in the nineteenth century.

Indigo is a very different kind of fiber-coloring agent than the majority of dyes of the eighteenth century. With most other dyes, a liquid bath is prepared and the fiber or yarn to be colored is cooked or dipped until the desired color is achieved. With indigo, a chemical reaction is started in a dye vat. The catalyst used to start the chemical reaction in an eighteenth-century indigo vat was a product called sig. Sig is stale human urine. (We here in the Weave Room are not quite eighteenth-century enough to use this catalyst. Instead, we use thiourea dioxide.)

The fiber or yarn to be colored is submerged in the liquid for about 20 minutes. When removed, it will be about the same color it was when it was put in the liquid. After about 20 minutes, the oxygen in the air will react with the dye solution and the fiber will begin to turn yellow. Shortly thereafter the yellow fiber will turn blue. This first dipping will produce a very light blue. In order to make it a darker blue, this procedure must be repeated. The more of these dippings, the darker the blue will become. Indigo's ability to change the color of a fiber right before your eyes caused some civilizations to look upon it with an awe bordering on worship.

The Virginia Gazette Index 1736–1780 by Lester J. Cappon and Stella F. Duff, published by The Institute of Early American History and Culture in 1950, lists no less than 40 advertisements for the sale of indigo. In the December 2, 1773 edition of the Purdie & Dixon *Virginia Gazette*, McCall and Shadden of Tappahannock, Virginia, advertised *we have lately imported and shall continue to do so (if we find quick sales) genuine Old Barbados Cane Spirits which are selling off on the most reasonable terms. We have likewise Madeira, Calcavella and St. Michael's Wine, Rum, Loaf Sugar, Coffee, Indigo, etc.*

Dyeing Blue with Indigo

INGREDIENTS

- ✛ 1 tablespoon of indigo
- ✛ 3 tablespoons of sodium carbonate (soda ash)
- ✛ 1 tablespoon thio-urea dioxide
- ✛ 4 gallons of water
- ✛ Up to 3 pounds of wool yarn

YARN PREPARATION

Soak the yarn to be dyed in clean water for at least 72 hours. This will thoroughly wet all of the molecules of the yarn and make it more receptive to dyeing. Keep the yarn in this water bath until it is ready to be placed into the indigo vat.

DYE PREPARATION

Mix 1 tablespoon of indigo in a cup of warm water and set it aside. Mix 3 tablespoons of soda ash with 4 gallons of water and bring the mixture to 120° F. Add the well-mixed indigo to the water and soda ash mixture and stir for about 1 minute.

Mix gently to avoid introducing extra oxygen. Give the mixture about 15 minutes to work and stabilize. Sprinkle 1 tablespoon of thio-urea dioxide gently over the mixture, spreading it all over the surface. It should take 15 to 20 minutes for the necessary chemical reaction to start. You can tell the dye vat is working when just below the surface the liquid has turned a yellow-green. At this point the dye bath is ready to use. Be careful to maintain the dye bath temperature between 120° F and 130° F. Allowing the temperature to go above or below this range will cause the chemical reaction to stop and render the dye bath useless.

DYEING

For indigo dyeing, the temperature of the dye liquid should not be high enough to cause temperature shock which would cause shrinking or felting. Place the wet skeins of wool yarn into the dye vat one or two at a time. To avoid streaking, the yarn should be held off of the bottom and sides of the dye container. Allow the yarn to stay in the dye bath for 17 to 20 minutes. When removing yarn, be careful not to drip into the dye bath. Dripping will introduce oxygen and shorten the dye bath's useful life. Allow the yarn to hang in the open air for at least 20 minutes; it will oxidize and turn blue. To make the color darker, place the yarn back in the dye bath again and proceed as before. The more dippings into the dye bath, the darker the blue color of the yarn will become.

Dyeing Green with Fustic or Turmeric and Indigo

ighteenth-century documents concerning textile dyeing suggest that their authors put a good bit of effort into writing about the color green. Even though Mother Nature provides lots of green in every season, eighteenth-century English dyers never found any single substance to bring it into being on a textile.

In the writings of a handful of eighteenth-century dyers, it is recommended that the yarn be first dyed blue and then yellow. I prefer to put the blue on top of the yellow. In this manner the yellow is shielded from sunlight by the blue. You can try it both ways and decide for yourself.

This book includes instructions for two yellow dyes: fustic and turmeric. Either yellow dye will work. Twenty plus years of practicing with eighteenth-century dyes has slanted my opinion in favor of fustic in chip form.

Remember that the yellows you achieve here are not the final result. I suggest that you dye many shades of yellow for your first green project. This will give you an opportunity to get lots of shades of green.

YARN PREPARATION

Soak the yarn to be dyed in clean water for at least 72 hours. This will thoroughly wet all of the molecules of the yarn and make it receptive to dyeing. Add the alum to 3 to 4 gallons of room-temperature water and mix well. Place the yarn in the mixture and slowly bring it to a very gentle boil. Boil the yarn gently for 1 hour. The yarn should stay in this mordant (alum) bath until it is ready to be placed into the fustic dye bath.

FUSTIC BATH INGREDIENTS AND PREPARATION

- 10 ounces of fustic chips or sawdust
- 4 ounces of potassium aluminum sulfate (alum)
- 1 ounce of cream of tartar
- 4 ounces of Glauber's salt
- 6 to 8 gallons of water
- Up to 5 pounds of wool yarn

Place the fustic chips or sawdust in 3 to 4 gallons of clean water and mix well for about 1 minute. Allow this mixture to soak for at least 24 hours, then mix vigorously for about 1 minute. Bring the mixture to a gentle boil for at least 3 hours. More boiling will not hurt. The liquid must be strained to remove the fustic chips or sawdust. Line a strainer or colander with several layers of cheesecloth and pour the liquid

through this sieve. The fustic chips or sawdust that is strained out can be tied up in the cheesecloth making a "tea bag" and used to strengthen the yellow dye pot later, if necessary. To this strained mixture, add 1 ounce of cream of tartar and 4 ounces of Glauber's salt and mix well for about 1 minute. Bring the mixture back to a boil and boil gently for about 60 minutes. The liquid is now the dye bath and ready to receive the yarn. It may be necessary to allow this to cool before dyeing.

Keep in mind that the turmeric recipe on pages 61–63 can be substituted for the fustic yellow recipe above.

DYEING YELLOW FOR GREEN

It is important not to temperature-shock the yarn. The temperatures of the alum bath and the dye bath should be about the same when transferring the yarn. Rapid change in temperature will cause the wool yarn to shrink and felt. When ready to do the dyeing, place the yarn from the alum bath into the dye bath and slowly bring it to a gentle boil. Cook the yarn until the desired color is achieved.

The yarn should then be washed to remove any excess dye. To stay in the history of the recipe, I would suggest using a mild eighteenth-century soap such as Castile. For convenience in today's world, baby shampoo or Orvus paste will work well. Rinse the yarn in clean water until the rinse water is clear. Keep the washed yellow yarn in the clear rinse water until it goes into the indigo vat. Remember that all eighteenth-century yellow dyes are severely fugitive in sunlight. Do not store the yellow yarn in the sun.

PLACING THE BLUE DYE ON THE YELLOW WOOL YARN FOR GREEN

Place wet skeins of yellow wool yarn into the indigo bath one or two at a time. To avoid streaking, the yarn should be held off of the bottom and the side of the dye container. Allow the yarn to stay in the dye bath for 17 to 20 minutes. When removing the yarn, be careful not to drip into the dye bath. Dripping will introduce oxygen and shorten the indigo dye bath's useful life. Allow the yarn to hang in the open air for at least 20 minutes; it will oxidize and turn green. To place more blue on the yarn, put it back into the dye bath for an additional 12 to 20 minutes; then remove it and allow it to oxidize. The more you repeat this procedure, the darker the blue color on top of the yellow will become. The yarn should then be washed to remove any excess dye.

Remember that the blue dye can be placed on the yarn first using either of the two yellow dyes. If you choose to do the blue dyeing first, the yarn must be mordanted with the alum before it is dyed blue. Don't be afraid to experiment.

A BATH TO BRIGHTEN THE LUSTER OF THE GREEN YARN

This is an optional step that you may wish to try. I have done this on several occasions with varying levels of success. Wool yarn dyed green can be brightened a bit by placing it in an afterbath of alum and water. This bath should be prepared by mixing ½ cup of alum per 3 gallons of clean water. The water should be hot enough to place your hand in comfortably. The yarn should stay in this bath 20 to 30 minutes.

Logwood: *The Natural History of Carolina Florida and the Bahama Islands...*; by Mark Catesby; London; Printed for B. White; 1771; Lacertus viridis Jamaieensis; The Green Lizard of Jamaica; Lignum Campechianum; Logwood

Logwood
(Haematoxylum campechianum)

The Spanish were the first Europeans to encounter textiles colored with logwood, sometimes referred to as campeachy wood. They found the natives using it to color cloth in Mexico and South America in the sixteenth century. The Spanish tested it and began to market it throughout the known world. The heart of the campeachy tree produces dyes that will yield colors of black, brown, purple, blue, and gray. This wide range of colors is obtained by varying the handling of the wood, the choice of mordants, the choice of additives, and the preparation thereof. The best or strongest dyes are from sawdust, filings, or chips taken from the trees' heartwood.

The use of logwood as a dye in England dates to the reign of Queen Elizabeth I (1558–1603). However, logwood's use as a dye had a bumpy existence there. Shortly after its introduction, laws were enacted that strictly forbade its use on the grounds that it was fugitive (not colorfast).[12] The laws against the use of logwood as a dye came to an end in 1662 during the reign of Charles II,[13] and the dye soon found its way to England's North American colonies. Wool dyed with logwood will begin fading toward gray in about nine years.

An advertisement placed by James M. Galt in the *Virginia Gazette* published by Purdie & Dixon of October 24, 1771, lists logwood among the products available at his apothecary on Duke of Gloucester Street in Williamsburg, Virginia.

Dyeing Purple and Black with Logwood

INGREDIENTS

- 12 ounces of logwood chips or 8 ounces of logwood sawdust
- 4 ounces of potassium aluminum sulfate (alum)
- 4 ounces of Glauber's salt
- 1 ounce of cream of tartar
- 4 to 8 gallons of water
- Up to 5 pounds of wool yarn

YARN PREPARATION

Soak the yarn to be dyed in clean water for at least 72 hours. This will thoroughly wet all of the molecules of the yarn and make it receptive to dyeing. Add the 4 ounces of alum to 3 to 4 gallons of water at room temperature. Place the yarn in this mixture and slowly bring it to a very light boil. Boil the yarn gently for 1 hour. The yarn to be dyed should stay in this mordant (alum) bath until it is ready to be placed into the dye bath. It may be necessary to allow this to cool before dyeing.

MAKING A STRONG DYE BATH

Place the logwood sawdust or chips in 3 to 4 gallons of clean water and mix well for about 1 minute. Allow this mixture to soak for at least 24 hours and then mix vigorously for a bit more than a minute. Bring this mixture to a gentle boil for at least 1 hour (a few minutes more will not hurt). The liquid must be strained to remove the logwood sawdust or chips. Line a strainer or a colander with several layers of cheesecloth and pour the liquid through this sieve. The logwood sawdust or chips that are strained should be tied up in the cheesecloth to make a "tea bag." Save the logwood tea bag; it can be used to strengthen the dye bath later, if needed. To the strained dye, add 1 ounce of cream of tartar and 4 ounces of Glauber's salt. Mix well for about 1 minute. Bring the mixture back to a boil and boil gently for about 60 minutes. The liquid is now the dye bath and ready to receive the yarn.

MAKING A QUICKER AND WEAKER DYE BATH

Place the logwood sawdust or chips in several layers of cheesecloth so that the bits and pieces cannot sift through. Pour a cup of water over them. Allow the wet logwood to work for about 24 hours, although, as much as 72 hours won't hurt. Tie the cheesecloth up to make a tea bag. Place it in 3 to 4 gallons of clean water. Boil the mixture for at least 1 hour, then remove the tea bag but save it to adjust the color in this dye bath or to make another one. Add 1 ounce of cream of tartar and 4 ounces of Glauber's salt. Mix for about 1 minute. Bring the mixture to a boil. The liquid is now the dye bath and ready to be used.

DYEING

It is important not to temperature-shock the yarn. The temperatures of the alum bath and the dye bath should be about the same when transferring the yarn. Rapid change in temperature will cause the wool yarn to shrink and felt. When you are ready to do the dyeing, place the yarn directly from the alum bath into the dye bath and slowly bring it to a gentle boil. The dye bath will yield shades of purple and dark black, depending on the length of time the yarn is cooked. Cook the yarn until the desired color is achieved.

Madder: Plage 851: Rubia Peregrina or Madder from *English Botany; or, Cloured Figures of British Plants* by Sir James Edward Smith. London: Printed by Richard Taylor. 1832.

Madder
(Rubia tinctorum)

Madder is a perennial plant having small yellow flowers, whorled leaves, and a red root. It looks a good bit like mint. The root of the plant is the source of the dye. The earliest evidence of madder's use as a dye comes from India where a piece of cotton cloth dyed with madder was found and dated to the third millennium BCE. Traces of madder in linen were found in Tutankhamen's tomb.[14] Madder has a long history of use in Turkey, India, and Iran where it is still being used.

The Oxford English Dictionary lists madder in the context of dye in 1347. Many of the renowned British "Red Coats" were colored using madder in a three-step fermentation process known as Turkey Red. Note that the coats of the line soldiers (privates and corporals) were dyed in this manner, which caused them to have a brick hue. The British government paid for these coats. The coats of the British officers were dyed with more expensive cochineal and were, therefore, scarlet. The officers themselves paid for these coats.

Madder also had many medicinal uses. It was used to treat jaundice, hemorrhoids, melancholy, and palsy. Madder seeds, mixed with vinegar and honey, were administered in a liquid form for swelling of the spleen. Roots and leaves

were pressed together and placed on freckles and other skin discolorations in an attempt to eliminate them.

In eighteenth-century Virginia few, if any, dyers ever went through the months of working and waiting necessary to make Turkey Red. Madder will grow just about anywhere and will produce a brilliant orange easily. Because madder was easily grown and easy to work with, it was often used on plantations to dye cloth for slave clothing.

An advertisement in the Purdie and Dixon *Virginia Gazette* of April 11, 1771, places madder for sale at John Greenhow's store in Williamsburg.

Madder grows well in Virginia's climate and soil. Therefore, it is one of the few eighteenth-century dyes listed in this book that can properly be considered as both a plantation and a professional dye.

Dyeing Orange with Madder

INGREDIENTS

- 8 ounces of madder root
- 3 ounces of potassium aluminum sulfate (alum)
- ¾ ounce of cream of tartar
- 3 ounces of Glauber's salt
- 6 to 8 gallons of water
- Up to 3 pounds of wool yarn

YARN PREPARATION

Soak the yarn to be dyed in clean water for at least 72 hours. This will thoroughly wet all of the molecules of the yarn and make it receptive to dyeing. Add 4 ounces of alum to 3 to 4 gallons of water at room temperature. Place the yarn in the mixture and slowly bring it to a very light boil. Boil the yarn gently for 1 hour. The yarn should stay in this mordant (alum) bath until it is ready to be placed into the dye bath. It may be necessary to allow this to cool before dyeing.

MAKING THE DYE BATH

Place 8 ounces of madder root in the dye pot and cover with 3 to 4 gallons of clean water. Allow this to soak for at least 24 hours. After the soak, bring the mixture to a gentle boil for at least 3 hours; a few minutes more will not hurt. The liquid must be strained to remove the madder roots. Line a large strainer or a colander with several layers of cheesecloth and pour the liquid through this strainer. The madder roots that are strained out can be tied up in the cheesecloth to make a "tea bag," which can be used to strengthen the color of this dye bath later, if needed. To the strained dye, add 1 ounce of cream of tartar and 3 ounces of Glauber's salt. Mix well for about 1 minute. Bring this mixture to a gentle boil, then allow the liquid to cool. The liquid is now the dye bath and ready to use.

DYEING

It is important not to temperature-shock the yarn. The temperatures of the alum bath and the dye bath should be about the same when transferring the yarn. Rapid changes in temperature will cause the wool yarn to shrink and felt.

For the color orange, place the yarn directly from the alum bath into the dye bath and slowly bring it to about 160°F. This temperature will yield the best orange color. To achieve a flat red-orange color, boil the yarn in the dye. Cook the yarn until the desired color is achieved.

Dyeing Red with Cochineal and Madder

INGREDIENTS

- ✛ 8 ounces of cochineal
- ✛ 6 ounces of madder
- ✛ 6 ounces of potassium aluminum sulfate (alum)
- ✛ 1 ounce of cream of tartar
- ✛ 5 ounces of Glauber's salt
- ✛ 6 to 8 gallons of water
- ✛ Up to 5 pounds of wool yarn

YARN PREPARATION

Soak the yarn to be dyed in clean water for at least 72 hours. Add the alum to 3 to 5 gallons of room-temperature water and mix well. Place the yarn in the mixture and slowly bring it to a boil. Boil the yarn gently for an hour. Keep the yarn in this mordant (alum) bath until it is placed into the dye bath.

MADDER PREPARATION

Place the madder roots in the dye pot, cover them with 1¾ gallons of clean water, and allow them to soak for at least 24 hours. After soaking, bring the mixture to a gentle boil for at least 3 hours (a few minutes more will not hurt). Add water, if needed, during boiling to maintain the 1¾ gallons in the cooking pot. Strain the liquid by pouring it through several layers of cheesecloth. The madder roots that are strained out can be tied up in the cheesecloth to make a madder tea bag that can be used to strengthen the dye bath later, if needed.

COCHINEAL PREPARATION

Grind or crush the cochineal to a fine powder. Place the ground cochineal in 1¾ gallons of clean water and mix well for about 2 minutes. Allow the mixture to soak for at least 24 hours and then mix vigorously for about 1 minute. Bring the mixture to a gentle boil for at least 1 hour, a few minutes more will not hurt. Add water, if needed, during boiling to maintain the 1¾ gallons in the cooking pot. Strain the liquid by pouring it through several layers of cheesecloth. The cochineal that is strained out can be tied up in the cheesecloth to make a tea bag and used to strengthen the dye bath later, if needed.

MIXING THE MADDER AND COCHINEAL DYES

Add the madder dye to the cochineal dye in a pot large enough to hold both. To this mixture, add 1 ounce of cream of tartar and 4 ounces of Glauber's salt and mix well for about 2 minutes.

Bring the mixture to a boil and boil gently for about 70 minutes. The liquid is now the dye bath.

DYEING

The temperatures of the alum bath and the dye bath should be about the same when transferring the yarn. When ready to do the dyeing, place the yarn directly from the alum bath into the dye bath and slowly bring up the temperature. In the range of 160°F to 180°F, madder is the dominant dye and the bath will yield various shades of orange color. At a gentle boil madder goes toward a rust color and cochineal will cause the bath to yield shades of red. Cook the yarn until the desired color is achieved.

Walnuts

English Walnut *(Juglans regia)*

Black Walnut *(Juglans nigra)*

White Walnut Tree *(Juglans cinerea)*

*B*lack walnut is a native American tree and is mainly grown today for its produce (walnuts) and its wood. It survives well westward to Minnesota and Nebraska and from New England to the Gulf of Mexico. Black walnut trees can grow to a height of 60 feet or more and may live over 100 years.

Walnuts: *The Natural History of Carolina Florida and the Bahama Islands...*; by Mark Catesby; London; Printed for B. White; 1771.

The best dye resides in the husk or the rind of the nut. The husk is the green covering around the nuts. It can be detached before the nuts are fully ripe and used to produce brown dye or the entire nut can be boiled in water to accomplish the same end.

During the twentieth century, black walnut trees have been grown mainly for expensive furniture. The nuts, however, are harvested in large quantities and eaten, used in baked goods, ice creams, candies, and other foods.

The black walnut tree was introduced into Europe in 1629. It was and still is cultivated there

as a forest tree for its high-quality wood. It is more resistant to frost than the English walnut, but grows best in the warmer regions of Europe. Walnut in eighteenth-century Virginia was both a plantation and a professional dye.

William Grove noted in his 1732 travel journal that maple bark produced a purple dye, and walnut hulls a dark brown.

John Wily discusses walnut hulls used as a brown dye in his pamphlet *A Treatise on the Propagation of Sheep, the Manufacture of Wool, and the Cultivation and Manufacture of Flax, with Directions for Making Several Utensils for the Business,* printed in Williamsburg, Virginia, by J. Royle in 1765.

In the year 1669, John Winthrop (1638–1707), colonial governor of Connecticut, sent a report on dyeing both cotton and wool with the bark of the white walnut tree *(Juglans cinerea).*

Dyeing Brown with Walnuts

INGREDIENTS

- ✛ 8 ounces of walnut husks or 3 pounds of walnuts with husks

- ✛ 5 ounces of Glauber's salt

- ✛ 1 ounce of cream of tartar

- ✛ 6 to 8 gallons of water

- ✛ Up to 3 pounds of wool yarn

YARN PREPARATION

Soak the yarn to be dyed in clean water for at least 72 hours. This will thoroughly wet all of the molecules of the yarn and make it receptive to dyeing. Note: There is enough tannic acid in the walnut husks to adhere to the molecules of wool yarn without using a mordant. The yarn should stay in this water bath until it is ready to be placed into the dye bath. Be careful with walnut dye. It will dye and stain everything it touches, even you.

MAKING THE DYE BATH

Place the walnuts with the husks just as they have fallen from the tree or the removed husks in several layers of cheesecloth so that bits and pieces of the husks cannot sift through into the dye bath. Place the "tea bag" in 3 to 4 gallons of clean water. This needs to soak for at least 12 hours. Bring the temperature up slowly and boil for at least 1 hour, then remove the walnut tea bag. Add 5 ounces of Glauber's salt and 1 ounce of cream of tartar. Mix well. The liquid is now the dye bath.

DYEING

The temperatures of the soaking water and the dye bath should be about the same when transferring the yarn. Rapid changes in temperature will cause wool yarn to shrink and felt. When you are ready to do the dyeing, place the yarn directly from the water bath into the dye bath and slowly bring it to a gentle boil. Cook the yarn until the desired color is achieved. As always, remember that the color of wet yarn appears darker than when it is dry.

Glossary

Alum: Aluminum potassium sulfate. Used as a mordant when dyeing wool and often combined with cream of tartar.

Alkanet: The southern European plant *Alkanna tinctoria* (family *Boraginaceae*), having blue flowers and a blackish root from which a red dye is obtained, also referred to as dyer's bugloss and orcanet. The first mention was found in 1343, according to the *Oxford English Dictionary.*

Annatto: A dye obtained from the soft pulp covering the seeds of *bixa orellana*. Other names for this substance are annetto, rocou, bixin, and orean. Annatto is native to Central and South America, as well as Asia. Traditionally used for coloring butter and cheese, it was also used as a textile dye.

Aquafortis: The early scientific and still popular name of the nitric acid of commerce (dilute HNO_3), a powerful solvent and corrosive.

Attapulgite: Clay mineral, basic hydrous silicate of magnesium and aluminum, one of the active ingredients of fullers earth.

Batik: The word *batik* is derived from the Javanese word *membatik* which means drawing or painting on cloth. It is the general term that describes a form of wax-resist dyeing (See Wax-Resist Dyeing) on cotton cloth. The craft of batik making is renowned in Java.

Blue Vitriol: Copper sulfate ($CuSO_4$). A poisonous blue chemical used in textile dyeing, electroplating, fungicides, and wood preservatives.

Catalyst: A substance which, when present in small amounts, increases the rate of a chemical reaction or process, but which is chemically unchanged by the reaction; a catalytic agent.

Chrome: Potassium dichromate. Poisonous, a mordant used to achieve a bright luster on wool and silk. It is very caustic and dangerous to handle.

Cochineal: Dachtylopius coccus. A dye made of dried, crushed, and ground insect carcasses. These insects thrive on the cactus *Opuntia cochenillifera*. The female insects, heavily laden with eggs, yield the best dye and are easily harvested from the cactus because they are unable to fly.

Copperas: Ferrous sulfate ($FeSO_4 \cdot 7H_2O$), used in wool dyeing as a mordant. Copperas has a saddening effect on the luster of woolen and worsted goods.

Cream of Tartar: The common name for potassium hydrogen tartrate, often used in combination with alum as a mordant in eighteenth-century English dyeing.

Crocking: Synonym for the rubbing off of color when referring to fastness in dyed or printed fabric.

Dyeing: The process of coloring fibers, yarn, cloth, or other materials through immersion in a liquor containing either mineral, vegetable, animal, or synthetic chemical dye compounds together with other chemicals to fix the dye into the fiber.

Fastness: This term applies to the resistance to change or fading, either by water, washing with soap or detergent, or by daylight, which the dye possesses, sometimes referred to as color-fastness.

Finishing: The course of action that gives cloth its final appearance, as well as its final hand or feel. It includes all of the processes that cloth goes through after leaving the loom in preparation. See Fulling.

Folk-Art Dyeing: Dyeing of textiles outside of an industrial or manufacturing setting, usually done by non-professional dyers, most often using dyestuffs obtained from nearby surroundings.

Foment: To wash or bathe with warm or medicated lotions; the application of fomentations; to lubricate.

Fugacious: Apt to flee away or flit. See Fugitive.

Fugitive: Quickly fading or becoming effaced, perishable. The color a fugitive dye produces will not last.

Fulling: The process of cleansing and thickening cloth by beating and washing; also called milling. Fulling was an apprenticed trade in eighteenth-century English society.

Fuller's Earth: A clay-like dirt made up principally of hydrated aluminum silicates that contain metal ions such as magnesium, sodium, and calcium within their structure. Montmorillonite is the primary mineral in fuller's earth, but it contains some additional minerals: kaolinite, attapulgite, and palygorskite. The name fuller's earth originated in the textile industry where workers cleaned wool by kneading it in a mixture of fine earth and water to adsorb oil, dirt, and other contaminants.

Fustic: The name of two kinds of wood, both used for dyeing yellow: 1. The wood of the Venetian sumach (*Rhus cotinus*), commonly referred to as young or Zante fustic; 2. The wood of the *Chlorophora tinctoria* or *Maclura tinctoria* of America and the West Indies, commonly referred to as old fustic.

Gall: Outgrowths produced on oak trees caused by the action of insects, mostly of the genus *Cynips*. Oak galls were a good source of tannin for eighteenth-century dyers.

Glauber's Salt: Common name for sodium sulfate decahydrate. It occurs as white or colorless monoclinic crystals. Johann Glauber was the first to artificially produce the salt in or about 1656. Glauber's salt is water soluble; has a salty, bitter taste; and was used by eighteenth-century dyers to help textiles dye evenly and more uniformly.

Gum Ammoniac: A brownish-yellow gum resin, having an acrid taste, from the plant *Dorema ammoniacum*, of western Asia. Used in porcelain, ceramics, and in medicine as an expectorant and counter-irritant.

Indigo: *Indigofera tinctoria*. Indigo is a bush that produces a blue dye which comes from the leaves of a sub-tropical bush. The leaves are fermented, the sediment collected, dried, and ground. Indigo is a vat dye. Both the bush and the dye are called indigo.

Kaolinite: Hydrated aluminum disilicate. A common mineral formed by the alteration of other minerals, especially feldspar.

Kettle Dye: See Mordant Dye.

Kermes: Dried pregnant female bodies of the insect *Coccus ilicis,* gathered from a species of evergreen oak in South Europe and North Africa, and used in dyeing the color red. It was used widely by English dyers in the eighteenth century.

Logwood: The heartwood of an American tree *(Hæmatoxylon campechianum)* used in dyeing; called logwood because it was imported in the form of logs. Logwood yields shades of purple, gray, and black on wool.

Madder: An orange and red dye from the root of the Eurasian herbaceous perennial *rubia tinctoria.* The coloring material of the madder plant, alizarin, is in the roots. As a textile dye, it easily produces an orange color on wool. It is the primary ingredient used to produce Turkey Red on cotton and wool.

Montmorillonite: A group of clay-like minerals characterized by the capacity to expand when they absorb large quantities of water. These are used in fulling and finishing and are found in fuller's earth.

Mordant: Usually a metallic salt or a metallic compound used during the process of dyeing natural fibers. A mordant will attach itself to the molecules of the fiber and the dye will attach itself to the mordant. Alum is a relatively safe and commonly used mordant. Some of the other mordants used in eighteenth-century textile coloring are: chrome, copper, iron, tannic acid, and tin. Some of these substances are dangerous to people, animals, and the environment.

Mordant Dye: Also known as a kettle dye. A mordant dye requires a mordant to make it colorfast in water, light, and the atmosphere. The mordant that is used will dictate the final color a dye will produce.

Natural Dye: Dyestuffs obtained from vegetables, fruits, shellfish, and minerals.

Oil of Vitriol: Sulfuric acid. A highly corrosive acid made from sulfur dioxide, widely used in the chemical industry. Used as a mordant.

Palygorskite: A group of lightweight, fibrous clay minerals presenting extensive substitution of aluminum for magnesium. Found in fuller's earth and used in fulling and finishing.

Sig or Sigg: Stale human urine. This source of ammonia was used for many things by dyers. It was the catalyst for indigo vats.

Saddening: Darkening and reducing the luster of a textile.

Soda Ash or Washing Soda: Sodium carbonate (Na_2CO_3). This substance is dissolved in water to create an alkaline solution for dyeing blue with indigo.

Tannin: *(Acidum tannicum).* The most commonly used mordant for cellulose fibers such as cotton and linen. Tannic acid is a specific commercial form of tannin.

Thiourea Dioxide: A modern reducing agent that is used as a catalyst for indigo dyeing. A substitute for sig.

Tin: Salt of tin, stannous chloride. Tin will brighten colors of red, orange, and yellow on wool and silk. More than just a little bit of it makes wool and silk brittle. At the end of a dyeing, a pinch of tin added to a dye bath mordanted with alum will brighten wool yarns or cloth. Tin was seldom, if ever, used on cellulose fibers in eighteenth-century dyeing. It is, like all mordants, somewhat toxic.

Turmeric: *Curcuma domestica, Curcuma longa.* The rootstock of an East Indian plant or the powder made from it. Used in dyeing textiles, it yields shades of yellow. Like the majority of eighteenth-century yellow dyes, it is not colorfast when exposed to light.

Turkey Red: Named for the country, not the bird. The process called Turkey Red was so long and complicated that separate dyeing facilities were needed to do this type of dyeing. Madder red, in combination with oil or fat, and an alum mordant yielded a red color with a slight brick hue on wool.

Vat Dyeing: Vat dyes are insoluble in water so they require a catalyst to start a chemical reaction so the dye can get on the fiber. Indigo is a natural vat dye and has been used extensively for many centuries.

Walnut: For use in dyeing, the outer husk of the walnut is used to obtain shades ranging from beige to brown.

Wax-Resist Dyeing: Resist dyeing is the name of a number of methods of creating patterns during textile dyeing. Wax is used to resist or prevent the dye from reaching all the cloth area, creating a pattern.

Washing Soda: Sodium carbonate chemical compound. Sodium carbonate is a white, odorless powder that absorbs moisture from the air, has an alkaline taste, and causes water to be strongly alkaline (it changes the pH). Used when dyeing with indigo.

Weld: The plant *Reseda luteola* yields a yellow dye. Also, the dye obtained from this plant.

Woad: A blue dye-stuff prepared from the powdered and fermented leaves of *Isatis tinctoria.* Now generally superseded by indigo, in the preparation of which it is still sometimes used.

End Notes

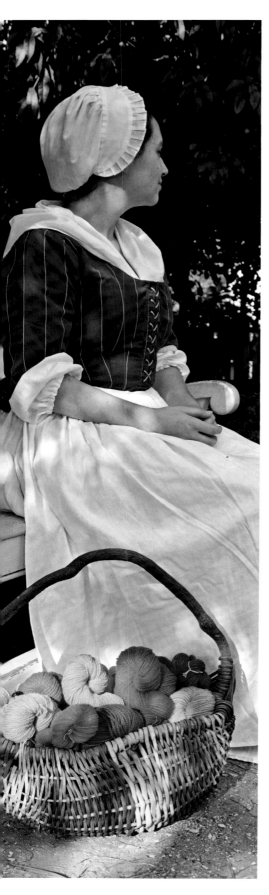

DYEING IN VIRGINIA

1. *Posselt's Textile Journal:* A Monthly Journal of the Textile Industries (March 1914, XVI), Publisher; Philadelphia: E.A. Posselt.
2. *Statutes of the Realm,* Vol. 5: 1628-80 (1819), page 425.
3. Thomas J. Wertenbaker; *The Planters of Colonial Virginia* (Princeton University Press, 1922)
4. *Virginia Gazette,* Purdie (July 1737) page 4; (September 21, 1739) 4.
5. *Virginia Gazette,* Rind (March 13, 1772) page 3, column 1.
6. William Ellis Jones, *Book and Job Printer, Annals of Augusta County, Virginia,* (Richmond, 1886) page 48.
7. *Virginia Gazette,* Purdie & Dixon (March 12, 1772) page 3, column 2.
8. *Robert Carter Letter Book 13* (Duke University Library) pages 129–30.

DYEING TOOLS

9. Blackley: An area of Manchester in Northwest England, 3.5 miles northeast of Manchester's center.
10. Excerpt from *"Pro Memoria-Turkey Red Dyeing and Blackley,"* a manuscript by W.H. Cliffe.

COCHINEAL

11. Amy Butler Greenfield, *A Perfect Red: Empire, Espionage, and the Quest for the Color of Desire* (New York: Harper-Collins, 2005).

LOGWOOD

12. John Harland, *Remains, Historical and Literary, Connected with the Palatine Counties of Lancaster and Chester* (Chetham Society: Manchester, England, 1863).
13. *Statutes of the Realm, Vol. 5: 1628-80* (1819) pages 393–400.

MADDER

14. David Jenkins, ed., *The Cambridge History of Western Textiles* (Cambridge University Press, 2003).

Bibliography

Adrosko, Rita J. *Natural Dyes in the United States.* *Washington, DC: Smithsonian Institution Press, 1968.*

Bemiss, Elijah. *The Dyer's Companion. New York: Dover Publications, 1973. Reprint of the 1815 edition published by E. Duyckinck: New York.*

Buchanan, Rita. *A Dyer's Garden: From Plant to Pot: Growing Dyes for Natural Fibers. Loveland, CO: Interweave Press, 1995.*

Cappon, Lester J. and Stella F. Duff. *The Virginia Gazette Index, 1736-1780. The Institute of Early American History and Culture, 1950.*

Chambers, Ephraim. *The Cyclopaedia or An Universal Dictionary of Arts and Sciences, 1st edition, 1728. Commonly referred to as Chambers Dictionary.*

Des Burslons, Jacques Savary. *The Universal Dictionary of Trade and Commerce, 3rd edition by Malachy Postlewayt, 2 volumes, printed in London in 1766. This book is often referred as Postlewayt's Dictionary.*

Ellis, Asa. *A Country Dyer's Assistant. Brookfield, Mass: E. Merriam and Co., 1798.*

Haigh, James. *The Dyer's Assistant in the Art of Dying Wool and Woolen Goods, extracted from the works of Mess. Ferguson, Dufay, Hellot, Geroffery, and Colbert. Translated from the French, 1778.*

Hargrove, John. *The Weavers Draft Book and Clothiers Assistant, with a new introduction by Rita J. Adrosko. Worcester: American Antiquarian Society, 1979. Reprint of the 1792 edition printed and sold by I. Hagerty, Baltimore.*

Johnson, Samuel. *Johnson's Dictionary of the English Language, 1st edition, 1755. This book is often referred to as Johnson's Dictionary.*

Liles, J. N. *The Art and Craft of Natural Dyeing: Traditional Recipes for Modern Use, Knoxville. University of Tennessee Press, 1990.*

Miller, Philip. *The Gardeners Dictionary: 1691–1771. Published in London, printed for the author, and sold by John and James Rivington, 1754.*

The Society of Gentlemen. *A New and Complete Dictionary of Arts and Sciences. Printed for W. Owen at Homer's Head in Fleet Street, London, in 1754. This book is sometimes referred to as Owen's Dictionary of Arts and Sciences.*

Wily, John. *A Treatise on the Propagation of Sheep, the Manufacture of Wool, and the Cultivation and Manufacture of Flax, with Directions for Making Several Utensils for the Business. Printed in Williamsburg, Virginia, by J. Royle in 1765.*

Worlidge, John and Nathan Bailey. *The Dictionarium Rusticum Urbanicum and Botanicum: A Dictionary of Husbandry, Gardening, Trade, Commerce and All Sorts of Country Affairs, 1st edition, 1704.*

About the Author

Max Hamrick is the weaving specialist and dyer for the Colonial Williamsburg Foundation. He is a third-generation Colonial Williamsburg employee and a sixth-generation textile worker. He has been making cloth for a living for nearly fifty years and has been dyeing professionally for 33 years.

Hamrick moved to Williamsburg, Virginia, when he was three years old. Before working for Colonial Williamsburg, he worked in the textile research and development department of Dow Badische Company.

About Colonial Williamsburg

The Colonial Williamsburg Foundation is a not-for-profit center for history and citizenship, encouraging audiences at home and around the world to learn from the past.

Colonial Williamsburg is dedicated to the preservation, restoration, and presentation of eighteenth-century Williamsburg, and the study, interpretation, and teaching of America's founding principles. In the Revolutionary City, the 301-acre restored eighteenth-century capital of Virginia, Colonial Williamsburg interprets the origins of the idea of America.

The Foundation actively supports history and citizenship education through a wide variety of outreach programs. These include Electronic Field Trips, which transport the story of our nation to students across the country; the Colonial Williamsburg Teacher Institute, which immerses elementary, middle, and high school teachers in interdisciplinary approaches to history and government; and The Idea of America™, a digital, interactive learning experience that brings American history to life and invites participants to look at history through the lens of key American values.

more AQS books

This is only a small selection of the books available from the American Quilter's Society. AQS books are known worldwide for timely topics, clear writing, beautiful color photos, and accurate illustrations and patterns. The following books are available from your local bookseller, quilt shop, or public library.

#8671

#1245

#8146

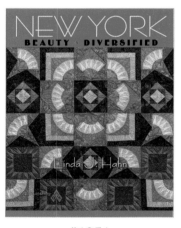

#1251

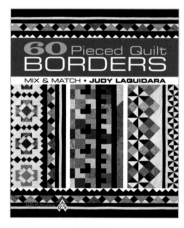

#8662

#8664

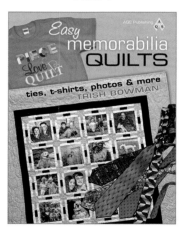

#1249

#8532

#1246

LOOK for these books nationally.
CALL or **VISIT** our website at

1-800-626-5420
www.AmericanQuilter.com